nature's
baby animals

BABY ANIMALS

OF LAKES AND PONDS

Carmen Bredeson

Dennis L. Claussen, PhD, *Series Science Consultant* Professor of Zoology, Miami University, Oxford, Ohio

Allan A. De Fina, PhD, *Series Literacy Consultant* Dean, College of Education/Department of Literacy Education, New Jersey City University, Jersey City, New Jersey; Past President of the NJ Reading Association

CONTENTS

WORDS TO KNOW

mute (myoot)—Not able to make any sound.

prey (pray)—An animal that is food for another animal.

rodent (ROH dent)—A type of animal with two large front teeth, such as rats, mice, and squirrels.

tadpole (TAD pohl)—A frog in the first part of its life.

LAKES AND PONDS

Ponds are LITTLE pools of fresh water.

Lakes are BIG pools of fresh water.

Many animals live in and around these waters. Baby animals have special ways to live and stay safe in ponds and lakes.

BABY **CAPYBARA**

The capybara is the biggest **rodent** in the world. A baby capybara [kah pee BAR uh] does not have a lot of hair. It rolls in the mud to cover its body. Then the capybara does not get a sunburn.

Mallard ducklings can swim right after they are born. They stay close to their mother in the water. Mallard ducks eat insects, fish, frogs, and plants. They put their heads deep in the water to find food.

BABY
MALLARD DUCK

BABY HIPPO

Hippos can stay under water for a LONG time!

A baby hippo is born under the water.
It comes up for its first breath of air.
Sometimes the baby crawls on its mother's
back. They take a little ride. Hippos spend
most of their lives in the water.

A baby frog is called a **tadpole**. Tadpoles look like little fish. They live in the water. Soon the tadpoles grow legs. Their tails get smaller and smaller. The tadpoles turn into frogs and hop, hop, hop onto land.

BABY FROG

BABY **TURTLE**

This turtle is a red-eared slider.

This baby turtle is about one inch long. It has red marks near its ears. Red-eared sliders live in the water. They crawl onto rocks to sit in the sun. When danger is near, they SLIDE into the water. Splash!

A baby **mute** swan is called a cygnet [SIG net]. Its parents are very big and strong. They protect their little cygnets from enemies. Mute swans make only a few hissing noises. Most of the time they are very quiet.

BABY
MUTE SWAN

BABY
RIVER OTTER

Baby otters like to play. They slide down
a mud bank and SPLASH into the water.
Otters swim very well. They can stay
under the water for eight minutes!
Their thick fur keeps them warm.

A baby heron [HEH run] is born in a nest. The nest is at the top of a tree. The chick learns to fly when it is two months old. Herons stand very still in the water. A fish or frog swims by. The heron catches the **prey** with its long beak.

BABY GREAT BLUE HERON

Books

Frog. New York: DK Publishing, 2007.

Hall, Margaret. *Herons*. Mankato, Minn.: Capstone Press, 2006.

Hatkoff, Isabella, Craig Hatkoff, and Paula Kahumbu. *Owen & Mzee: The True Story of a Remarkable Friendship*. New York: Scholastic Press, 2006.

Mara, Wil. *Otters*. New York: Marshall Cavendish Benchmark, 2007.

Mayer, Cassie. *Lakes and Ponds*. Chicago: Heinemann Library, 2007.

National Geographic. *Animals.*
<http://animals.nationalgeographic.com/animals>

San Diego Zoo. *Animal Bytes.* "Hippopotamus."
<http://www.sandiegozoo.org/>
Click on "Animals and Plants" and
select "Animal Bytes."
Then click on "Mammals."
Then click on "Hippopotomus."
   Hear hippo sounds.
   See hippo photos.

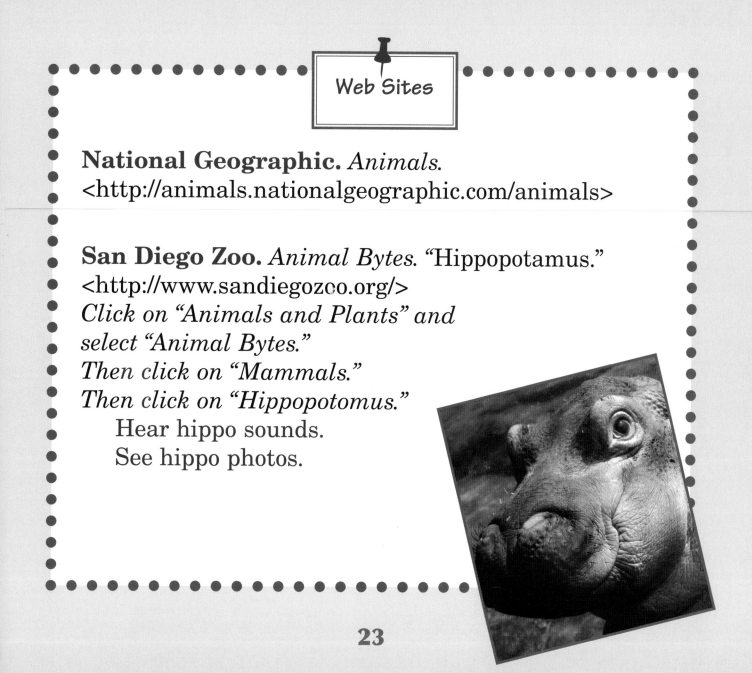

INDEX

~For Kate and Caroline, our beautiful granddaughters~

Enslow Elementary, an imprint of Enslow Publihshers, Inc.
Enslow Elementary® is a registered trademark of Enslow Publishers, Inc.

Library of Congress Cataloging-in-Publication Data

Bredeson, Carmen.
    Baby animals of lakes and ponds / Carmen Bredeson.
        p. cm. — (Nature's baby animals)
    Includes bibliographical references and index.
    Summary: "Up-close photos and information about baby animals of lakes and
ponds"—Provided by publisher.
    Library Ed. ISBN 978-0-7660-3563-8
    Paperback ISBN 978-1-59845-224-2
    1. Lake animals—Infancy—Juvenile literature. 2. Pond animals—Infancy—Juvenile
literature. I. Title.
    QL146.B74 2011
    591.763—dc22   2009037899

Printed in the United States of America
102010 Lake Book Manufacturing, Inc., Melrose Park, IL

10 9 8 7 6 5 4 3 2 1

♻ Enslow Publishers, Inc., is committed to printing our books on recycled paper. The paper
in every book contains 10% to 30% post-consumer waste (PCW). The cover board on the out-
side of each book contains 100% PCW. Our goal is to do our part to help young people and
the environment too!

Every effort has been made to locate all copyright holders of material used in this book. If any
errors or omissions have occurred, corrections will be made in future editions of this book.

Photo Credits: *Animals Animals:* © Leo Keeler, pp. 2 (otter), 18, © Patti Murray, p. 6;
© Bernard Castelein/naturepl.com, p. 20; © Ferrero-Labat/Auscape International, p. 11;
iStockphoto.com: © Andy Gehrig, p. 8, © Evelin Elmest, p. 3 (children), © Tommounsey,
p. 3 (tadpole); Michael S. Quinton/Getty Images, p. 21; *Minden Pictures:* © Konrad Wothe,
p. 15, © Michael & Patricia Fogden, pp. 1, 14, © Rob Reijnan/Foto Natura, p. 16, © Stephen
Dalton, p. 12, © Theo Allofs, p. 7, © ZSSD, pp. 10, 23; © Pete Oxford/naturepl.com, p. 19;
© Oxford Scientific/Photolibrary, pp. 2 (tadpole), 13; Photos.com, p. 3 (egret, squirrel);
Shutterstock, p. 5; © Wildlife/Peter Arnold, Inc., p. 17; © Woodfall/Photoshot, p. 9.

Cover Photo: © Wildlife/Peter Arnold, Inc.

Note to Parents and Teachers: The *Nature's Baby Animals* series supports the
National Science Education Standards for K–4 science. The Words to Know section
introduces subject-specific vocabulary words, including pronunciation and definitions.
Early readers may need help with these new words.

Enslow Elementary
an imprint of
Enslow Publishers, Inc.
40 Industrial Road
Box 398
Berkeley Heights, NJ 07922
USA
http://www.enslow.com